A Cop's Guide to Lower Manhattan

By Det. Ike Ilkiw (NYPD, Ret.)
and
Aaron Arnout

ISBN: 0988909103

ISBN-13: 978-0-9889091-0-6

The cover artwork was created by
Jay French, of Jay French Studios.

www.NYCAdventureTours.com

Photos by Dale Mary Fitzgerald

A Note From Ike

After I retired from the NYPD, I tried several different jobs, but the one I've enjoyed the most is running my own tour guide company, NYC Adventure Tours. People would often ask me how I came upon all this knowledge and trivia that I would share during my tours and I always had a simple explanation: I love New York. It's as simple as that. I simply love the place. I count myself the luckiest person in the world because I was born here, and with any luck, I will probably die here.

My love and affection for New York is an unconditional one, as any true romance should be. I know that New York has many faults and that some things aren't very nice, but I can still say that I am crazy about this place. Every day I spend here is a blessing.

When I told my friends I was working on this book with Aaron, they said, "Big deal—every street corner in New York is a crime scene."

This book is about those street corners, and about these crime scenes.

- Det. Ike Ilkiw (NYPD, Ret.)

TABLE OF CONTENTS

For the purposes of this book, the term 'Lower Manhattan' refers to Manhattan south of 14th Street, from the Hudson River to the East River. The locations are listed geographically walking north to south.

THE EAST VILLAGE

Tompkins Square Park
East 7th to East 10th between Avenues A and B

Tompkins Square has always been a kind of barometer for Alphabet City and the Lower East Side as a whole. Once, not so long ago, it was littered with needles and the people who used them. Drug use has always been a part of New York City's culture, but the twin epidemics of heroin and freebase (crack) cocaine made previous drug waves pale in comparison. To put it bluntly, the fourteen years between 1981 and 1995 didn't exactly present the best public face of our fair city.

In fact, the Lower East Side was still artsy, but in a way that made the free-love, do-as-thou-shalt Roaring Sixties look like the era had been run over by a biker gang. Maybe it had been—and that gang's name was Punk. The movement rejected anything but nihilism and attracted the downtrodden, the young-and-politically active, rock n' rollers, squatters, anarchists, drug dealers, and anybody who had a beef with 'The System.' The nerve center of the filthy underside of that world was Tompkins. It's since been heavily policed and cleaned up to a fraction of its former level, and is now a genuinely nice place to go for a walk.

What's Historical?

The Park has also borne witness to tragedy ancient and dour: in the summer of 1904, a steamboat called the *General Slocum* caught fire and sank in the East River in shallow water. On board were nearly fifteen hundred people, mainly German immigrants headed to a Lutheran church picnic. Over a thousand people were confirmed dead from that single accident, which largely led to the dissolution of the 'Little Germany' community in Manhattan's Lower East Side as a direct result of the loss of so many prominent members and social leaders in the German community.[i] In the park, you can see a touching memorial fountain dedicated to the children who died on the *General Slocum* disaster:

IKE SEZ: 151 Avenue "B: between East 9 and 10th street was once the home of bebop musician Charlie Parker, who lived here from 1950 until his death in 1955. It is designated a National Historic Site. Also, Williamsburg gangster 'Lucky' Luciano's first home when his family came to America was at 265 East 10th Street.[ii] Small world.

Movies and Television:

The park was a filming location for Die Hard 3, (1995) and the bar at the corner of 7th Street and Ave. "B" was a filming location for Crocodile Dundee (1986).

Second Ave Deli (Former location)

East 10th St. and Second Ave.

I worked this case. Nobody knows who shot Abe Lebewohl. Well, *somebody* knows, but that person isn't saying anything. The old man was from the Ukraine, and had survived the Einsatzgruppen, the pogroms, the Gestapo and the SD. Then he got put into a death camp and survived that. When he got to Manhattan, head held high, he worked hard until he was able to open his deli. This was in 1954. For more than forty years, he served great food to the neighborhood and made hundreds of lifelong friends. On March 4th, 1996, he was walking to a bank on 6th Street when someone shot him dead. His deli later moved to 162 East 33rd Street, where it remains today.

Because I speak Ukrainian, and the neighborhood around Veselka and the Lys Mykyta remains a pocket of Ukrainian speakers (the Ukrainian National Home is there, too), I was assigned this case. I put up a great deal of posters in Ukrainian and English with a description of the crime.

On East 10th Street and 2nd Ave, there is a small cobblestone park in front of the church, dedicated to his name and the meaning of his memory.

What's Historical?

Directly across the street from what once was the Second Avenue Deli is the St. Marks on the Bowery Church; at 131 east 10th Street. The church yard contains the remains of New York's first governor, Peter Stuyvesant, when this town was still called New Amsterdam, and businessman A.T. Stewart. Stewart was an incredible man; along with his businesses, he incorporated what would later become the Long Island Rail Road, and the town of Garden City in Nassau County. Incredibly, after his death in 1876, his remains were stolen and held for ransom. The ransom was paid, but the remains were never conclusively identified as being A.T. Stewart.

Police Athletic League
34 ½ East 12th Street, between Broadway and University Place.

The police are not only here to help catch robbers and killers and to maintain order. After a long career in the Department, I am firmly of the opinion that the police forces of our nation's cities help reinforce the ties that bind society together in its most basic sense. I'll be the first to say that some cops join for the wrong reasons; some cops stay for still others. But the vast majority of police officers in New York City are strong, good, community-minded men and women who work hard for very low pay to help keep our city stay safe so we can do business and raise families in peace. One of the best things to come out of the Department's more egalitarian initiatives has been the Police Athletic League.

Founded in 1915, the League fosters a sense of organization and well-being (both in a mental and physical sense) in the youths and families it touches. Funded to a large degree by donations, the League has done an important job of helping give youths who would otherwise be running with criminal elements the benefit of the doubt and providing them with opportunities to enter social circles that would otherwise be closed to them.

Recent initiatives and donations have come from prosecutors—one such case in the Bronx led to the funding of a youth center with the proceeds from confiscated cash from drug raids.[iii]

The Post Office, located nearby on Broadway, was a filming location for *Seinfeld*; it's the exterior shot for episodes involving Newman.[iv]

What's Historical?

Just around the corner on East 11th Street stands a relatively modern building that looks out of place in the neighborhood. This building was once the residence of **Leon Klinghoffer**; a retired business man who was a passenger on the ill fated ***Achille Lauro.*** On October 7, 1985 he was shot to death by terrorists who had taken over the ship in a bid to free other imprisoned terrorists.

The Cannibal Killer
700 East 9th Street

By the time Dan killed his girlfriend and made soup from her body, he knew he was destined for great things. He looked a little like Kurt Cobain, but dressed kind of preppy—long buttoned shirts and shaggy blond hair. Sunglasses. An easy smile. Dan Rakowitz knew his cannabis—he grew it out in Texas. When he moved to the East Village in the mid-Eighties, he showed up with plenty of it. Additionally, he happened to have a not-so-firm grasp on reality. He had religious delusions and thoughts of grandeur, fancying himself a leader of sorts.

Eventually, his magnetism and unpredictable nature got and lost him a 19 year-old girlfriend named Monica Beerle. She was a Swiss dance student.

He said her brains tasted "pretty good." He put her bones in a plastic bucket and left them in Port Authority, and then served soup to the homeless. Her soup. He made it in this apartment, at 700 E. 9th Street, on August 19th, 1989.[v] Word on the street says the building recently had bedbugs, which might to many New Yorkers be a bigger horror than involuntary cannibalism.

What a model citizen! Not many people in these fast-moving modern times share Daniel Rakowitz's civic drive to help others. The courts, after some deliberation, thought he could do his best work for the community out in Kirby Forensic Psychiatric Center, on Wards Island. There, he claims he'll be the youngest person ever elected President.

He gets checked in on, now and then, but it's safe to say he's probably not coming out. A 2004 investigation by a Manhattan jury found him 'no longer dangerous,' but still creepy enough to need to stay inside. A man can dream, can't he?

Ike Sez:

Oh, by the way, take a walk over to 173 Ave. "C" and look up to the third floor: It's where my Mom and Dad, and my oldest brother lived when they first came to America in 1951.

Former site of the "Binibon Restaurant"

Northwest Corner; Second Ave., and 5th Street.

We've all had to use a restroom in Manhattan. It's tough.

Not everyone is willing to go the lengths Jack Abbott did to get into one. He had a second chance, but he really needed to use that bathroom, and was willing to kill to get to it.

Norman Mailer knew this guy. Jack Henry Abbott. Isn't it funny how only murderers have middle names, usually? Jack had a hard life and evidence indicates that he was not in the habit of taking guff from anybody. When he was twenty-one, he was doing hard time for forgery in Utah. He shanked another prisoner to death with an improvised knife and caught a manslaughter charge for it—the state slammed another three to twenty on him. I can't see how they'd be that lenient today. At any rate, his letters got the attention of none other than Norman Mailer, and with that author's help he published a book about doing time, *In the Belly of the Beast*.[vi] Oh, and Abbott got out.

When he was released from prison he came to New York like a literary god. Manhattan has always had a fascination with deviants—after Burroughs, Ginsberg, and the like, Abbott was a passable diversion for the literati looking for something new, something edgy. Something dangerous. For the few weeks of freedom he had on his return, he was the toast of the town. Things were looking up. Unfortunately, he didn't leave his thuggish methods of settling scores back in prison, and quickly spoiled the whole 'reformed criminal turned artist' image by messing up the 'reformed' part.

Needing to use a restroom, Jack came to this restaurant (then called the Binibon) and argued with Richard Adan.

Richard was the 22-year old son of the owner of the place, and had the unenviable task of telling Jack that the restrooms were for employees only.

Jack stabbed him to death right there.[vii] Locked up immediately, he ended up never gaining notoriety for his writing again and died a prison suicide in 2002.[viii] Ironically, Adan was an up-and-coming writer whose first play had just been approved for production.

IKE SEZ:

Norman Mailer once lived at 41 First Avenue, just up the block. Small world!

NYPD 9th Precinct
321 East 5th Street.

In the late 1960s and early 1970s, reactionary elements in American society (such as the Weather Underground and the Black Panthers) advocated various forms of armed revolutionary change against a government they perceived to be illegitimate. Although none of these organizations were successful in overthrowing the United States Federal Government, many of them made a name for themselves striking blows of insurrection against what they saw to be the ills of society.

Two young men who had just returned from Vietnam (where they had served together as Marines) were placed together in the East Village in 1972 on a foot patrol out of the 9th Precinct. They went to a diner on Eleventh Street and Avenue B. They made it outside after eating only to be ambushed by what investigators believe were black militants with guns. Rocco Laurie (age 23), of Staten Island, and Gregory Foster (age 22), of the Bronx, died on the scene an hour before midnight on January 27th, 1972. The case remains unsolved, unfortunately.[ix]

Movies and Television:

The stone face of this precinct stationhouse has appeared in the film *Glitter*[x], as well as in at least four television shows: *NYPD Blue*[xi], *Castle*[xii], *Kojak*[xiii], and *Cagney and Lacey*[xiv].

IKE SEZ:

The militants of yesteryear would be surprised to see how glitzy the East Village has become today! Formerly gritty areas of the city are now glamorous and filled with high rise condos and expensive boutiques. What would the Weather Underground make of that?

Nicole DuFresne Murder

Corner of Rivington and Clinton Streets

In the early morning hours of January 27, 2005 Nicole duFresne was walking with her friends on Clinton Street on the Lower East Side. Less than a mile away, another group of friends were still full of energy after a few hours spent playing video games—they went out to 'mess with people.' One of them, Rudy Fleming, had brought a gun.

When the two groups moved close to one another, Nicole and her friends laughing and chatting in the cold air, Rudy produced a revolver which had been used by him earlier in the night to rob a 22-year old security guard of his leather jacket.

It started, as so many things do, with one small step at a time.

Rudy confronted the group. When he didn't get what he wanted right away, he pistol-whipped Nicole's fiancé, Jeffrey Sparks, and grabbed one of the girls' purses. Foolishly, Nicole did the thing no one faced with an armed assailant should do unprepared: she verbally confronted him. "What are you going to do, shoot us?" she is remembered as saying. Rudy Fleming tried to shoot Nicole's friend Mary Jane, but the gun misfired. Quickly pulling the trigger again, he discharged one .357 round into Nicole's chest. She died in the arms of her fiancé.

Multiple arrests were made in this case, of both the principal suspect, Fleming (murder in the first degree), as well as the other members of his group on lesser charges. Rudy Fleming was sentenced to life without parole as a result of the charges levied against him.[xv] Fleming's girlfriend, who assisted in the robbery, got a second-degree murder charge.

A promising writer, Nicole duFresne has had her work produced posthumously.

WEST VILLAGE

Jefferson Market Courthouse

425 Sixth Ave. Corner of West 9th Street.

It's funny, thinking about how things might have been. I'm not a necessitarian or even a philosopher—hell, I'm a cop. Things are the way they turned out, and life's too short to ask yourself what maybe *could've* happened. But sometimes I can't help myself. So here goes: cops used to not be so honest in New York City. Although the Department's checks and balances (as well as Internal Affairs divisions) are pretty stringent and watchful now, things didn't always use to be this way. There used to be a lot of dirty cops—just ask Frank Serpico.

Jefferson Market Courthouse (built in 1883, named after President Thomas Jefferson) is a beautiful structure—we'll get to that. What's *really* interesting, though, is what one trial perhaps caused. You see, the racy film star and playwright Mae West went on trial in 1927 for producing an 'obscene' play, *Sex*. Although pretty tame by today's standards, the work got her charged with a serious crime. She was tried here, at Jefferson, and spent the whole time thinking she'd get off scot-free thanks to her fancy Tammany lawyer. She didn't. This was due to a large degree to the media attention the trial attracted.

A reporter, one of the legions sent to interview West, happened upon another female prisoner and had a brief talk. The prisoner told her story: she had been set up (I've heard that one a lot). She hadn't played 'by the rules' – she refused to give the required kickback to a vice cop. This little revelation blew up the front pages and eventually sparked a separate institutional investigation, the Seabury Commission.[xvi] That Commission, headed by Samuel Seabury, took testimony about dirty police and dirty courts from over a thousand people. Hundreds of hours of interviews were conducted. The fallout from the investigation rocked New York all through the early Thirties and led directly to the resignation of then-Mayor Jimmy Walker. This led directly to the instatement of legendary leader Fiorello LaGuardia as mayor. Mae West caused LaGuardia to become Mayor? You be the judge.

The Courthouse (now a City Library) rises from the earth phoenix-like from Sixth Avenue, its red brick drawing the eye pleasantly upwards. The work possesses splendidly beautiful, effective examples of Venetian Gothic details in the stained glass windows and the clock tower itself.

Stonewall Inn
53 Christopher Street between Seventh Ave. and Waverly Place.

Stonewall is a legendary word among the LGBT (lesbian, gay, bisexual and transgender) communities in America. At the height of what the Haight/Ashbury would call the Summer of Love, in late June 1969, Greenwich Village's Stonewall Inn blew up. I don't mean a literal explosion, like what happened on Wall Street in 1920 or in Fraunces Tavern in 1975, but the effects were perhaps further reaching than any act of terror. This was an act of hope, and of rebellion. A police raid in the early hours of the morning on the Inn netted a few arrests for indecency and drugs and so on. In this, there was nothing remarkable.

What the task force hadn't counted upon was the immediate, spontaneous public backlash. The violent demonstrations were prompt and widespread among the gay- and gay-friendly community of the Stonewall. There existed in police culture at that time an unfortunate bent toward the persecution of sexual and ethnic minorities in New York. The community had simply taken enough abuse. On that sweltering June night, they fought back and played a game of hit-and-run with the police, who summoned backup. Although the crowd dispersed eventually, the "Stonewall Riots," as they came to be known, became a watershed moment for the gay community nationwide.[xvii] These acts of institutional defiance became a rallying cry and an act of inspiration for the oppressed members of the LGBT community everywhere, and helped spark the nascent gay rights movement. The Stonewall Inn has since been designated a National Historic Landmark.

What's Historical?

Directly across the street from the Stonewall Inn is Christopher Park with an imposing statue of General Sheridan of the Union Army, and Segal's Gay Pride Sculptures. Just around the corner, at the intersection of Christopher Street., Grove Street and Waverly Place is the Northern Dispensary. Founded in 1827, and built in 1831 it was where **Edgar Allan Poe** went for medical care.

Triangle Shirtwaist Factory
23-29 Washington Place, Bewteen Greene and Washington Square East.

It started, as so many things do, very slowly. A smoldering spark licked into flame in the huge, misshapen nest of fibers in a scrap bin underneath a cutter's table. The Triangle Factory made shirts in a sweaty, intimate, closed-door environment. The management, unfortunately for everyone, also 'ran a tight ship.' In 1911, that meant they locked everybody in so they couldn't duck out for a quick smoke. Because the doors were chained shut, the fatalities were extensive—one hundred forty six people died as a result of the fire, six of them remaining unidentified until 2011. The majority of the victims perished from burns or asphyxiation. The fire made headlines and triggered a citywide crackdown on fire code violations. The Factory site is now a New York City and National Landmark.[xviii]

18 West 11th Street.

The radical Weather Underground wanted to make a statement. Unfortunately, all they succeeded in doing was making a statement about the fact that they didn't know how to handle dynamite. And they almost killed Dustin Hoffman, (he lived next door to the clandestine factory, with his wife, and had just completed "Midnight Cowboy").

The bombs they were assembling, simple antipersonnel shrapnel devices with electric fuses, were essentially pipes filled with nails and dynamite. It took investigators more than a week just to determine how many people had died in the blast. It's not clear why the bombs detonated when they did (at the West Village townhouse rather than at Fort Dix, NJ or at Columbia University), but it killed three Weather Underground members: Diana Oughton, Theodore Gold, and Terry Robbins.

Two women who were upstairs were only lightly injured and stunned: Cathlyn Wilkerson and Kathy Boudin. They managed to get to a neighbor's house after first responders found them. Active members of the Weather Underground, they slipped through the ever-widening Federal net which had begun to close around them.

They remained fugitives for more than ten years—Wilkerson turned herself in in 1980, and Boudin was caught in an armored car robbery the next year.[xix]

14 West 10th Street.

I'd like to think he started out a good man. Perhaps we all start as good people. I don't know. Freebasing cocaine is a terrible decision anyway, but Joel Steinberg got violent and controlling when he did it. By the time he finished his Air Force career, Joel was headed for a future as a lawyer. Veterans had provision during this time in New York to skip the bar exam if they wished, and Joel became a practicing lawyer in 1970. Unfortunately, his subsequent decisions proved to not be so fortuitous. The crack was just the beginning of it: he became heavily involved in a violent, sadomasochistic relationship with his live-in partner, Hedda Nussbaum. While there's nothing wrong with relations between consenting adults, he allegedly caused permanent physical damage to her spinal column, and he definitely broke her face with a series of hard punches at some point. When this dream couple decided to illegally adopt a child, Elizabeth, harsh reality came crashing down all around them. A punch went awry, or he aimed one at the child—either way, Elizabeth ("Lisa") was hit, and lay on a hard floor for at least eight hours until she went into respiratory arrest. It was only at this point that the couple called 911, with Joel coaching Hedda through the call. Her voice sounded at once throaty and strangely nasal, but the authorities found it wasn't because of stress. When first responders came to Apartment 3W, it was locked— a strange situation for a family in urgent need of an ambulance. Hedda slowly opened the door, and shocked investigators with her appearance: she had two black eyes, her lip was split open and bleeding, and her nose was completely broken and crushed. He went at her like something out of *Raging Bull*. That was why her voice sounded so strange.

The child was not as lucky as Hedda – Lisa died after being taken off life support some days later. The swelling in her brain had killed her. Joel had beaten her to death.

On January 30, 1989, Joel Steinberg was convicted and was and given the maximum sentence; 8 ½ to 25 years in prison.[xx] He was repeatedly denied parole because he showed zero remorse for the crime, and still maintains his innocence. He now reportedly lives on 123rd Street and works in construction.

IKE SEZ:

Mark Twain lived in the same building back in 1900. He was somewhat better behaved than Joel. Dashiell Hammett, writer of the masterpiece “The Maltese Falcon,” lived at 28 West 10th Street. Two and a half blocks away, across Greenwich, is James M. Cain’s old residence at #11 Charles Street. His classic, “Double Indemnity,” is considered a sterling example of the thriller genre and has been successfully translated multiple times into cinema.

86 Bedford, Between Barrow and Grove Street. Chumley's, former bar and speakeasy.

Chorley's was a famous and very old New York classic speakeasy located at 86 Bedford Street. During Prohibition, the place provided privacy and discretion to its clientele, as well as an escape route: it had an entrance through an interior adjoining courtyard. The police were on the bar's payroll; when there was a raid coming, a corrupt cop would call ahead, sometimes only minutes before the squad arrived to investigate. When that occurred, the bartender would give a shout for everyone in the establishment to "EIGHTY-SIX!" when meant everyone inside should immediately run out the entrance to the bar at 86 Bedford Street, because the police were coming through the courtyard door. It isn't clear that this is the origin of the restaurant term "eighty-six" (to be out of something, or to throw someone out of an establishment), however. Michael Quinion's incisive work on the subject shows several possible alternate origins for the phrase.[xxi]

PLEASE NOTE: This information is about the location only. At the time of this printing, he building is being renovated and the future of Chumley's is unclear. Stay tuned.

IKE SEZ:

The West Village is one of the most picturesque parts of Lower Manhattan, and almost every street and avenue has appeared in hundreds of movie and television shows; just a few steps away is **75 ½ Bedford Street** which just might be the narrowest house in New York City. It's only 9 ½ feet wide and was once home to the likes of poet **Edna St. Vincent Millay**, actors **John Barrymore** and **Cary Grant**. Also, walk south to Seventh Ave., turn right on Leroy street and continue to St. Luke's Place and you'll find #10 St. Luke's Place which was the filming location for the exterior shot of "The Cosby Show". The entire block has appeared in movies like "Autumn in New York" and episodes of "Law and Order". The building at the corner of Grove and Bedford is used in the exterior shots of the "Friends" TV show, and the café on the ground level was (I am told) the inspiration for the "Central Perk" café where the "Friends" meet.

Frank Serpico's Basement Apartment
116 Perry Street

Frank Serpico joined the NYPD in 1959. He wanted to be a cop, especially an honest cop. He never took a bribe, never compromised his morals in any way, and is one of the most famous government whistleblowers in New York.

He was a grunt uniformed patrol officer for more than a decade, and never got very close to any of his co-workers. When he started working plainclothes, after fourteen years on the job, Serpico found that many of his fellow officers, especially the plainclothes detectives, were more or less compromised by criminal elements. They took bribes, falsified evidence, didn't follow safeguards and regulations, and generally were just as corrupt as the criminals they put behind bars. Serpico's experience as an investigator was made difficult because not only did he never take a bribe, he told his commanders when he knew that other officers did.

He embarrassed a lot of people and the management promoted him to detective. He was sent to a heroin house in Williamsburg, Brooklyn on Driggs and South 4th. His two partners didn't come to the door with him like they were supposed to—instead, they let Frank go to the door alone, with no backup, and try to force his way in.

Someone shot him in the face through the door; his partners saw everything but refused to help him. Finally an old man came, saw him bleeding there on the street, and called an ambulance for him. When he was in the hospital, his fellow police wouldn't let him rest, coming and checking his bed every hour to wake him up. "For safety," they said. Really, it was just continuing harassment. You see, they hated Frank Serpico.

He got a medal for heroism, the Medal of Honor, for his efforts.

The misadventure with the getting-shot-in-the-face part came about eight or nine months after his front-page New York Times story about police corruption went public.

After he recovered, he continued to testify against the corruption endemic in the Department.

. Furthermore, he put his own life behind his ideals, routinely exposing himself to death threats and risk at the hands of his fellow police officers.[xxii] His efforts led to the anti-corruption efforts of the Knapp Commission, led by William Knapp.

208 Sullivan St: Triangle Civic Improvement Association

Vincent Gigante, the boss of the Genovese crime family, lived across the street with his mother. He pretended to be incompetent or crazy from the 1960s onward, though the act didn't really get to be 24/7 until the 80s. In the dark, dusty environs of the club, Vincent and his most trusted men would sit and play pinochle into the evening on long afternoons. They said little outside of whispers, but somehow Gigante remained on top of up-to-the-minute information about the goings-on of his organization even as the Federal Bureau of Investigation relentlessly watched his every move.[xxiii]

Nowadays, the building is closed, and has been for years. The gate is down and locked.

225 Sullivan Street: Vincent Gigante's childhood home

Vincent Gigante pretended to be crazy for more than forty years. He would shuffle around Greenwich Village in a bathrobe and slippers, talking to himself—seemingly yet another harmless but batty man in New York City.

225 Sullivan Street was his mother's house; most mornings he would emerge in either a bathrobe and slippers or a light pullover and a pair of ratty trousers. Accompanied by a bodyguard or two, he would cross the street to the Triangle Club, and spend a few hours playing pinochle and whispering to his trusted associates. As boss (having wrested control from Frank Costello back in the 1960s), he

implemented strict security measures. Nobody in the organization could say his name or his nickname over the phone. If they had to refer to him, they pointed to their chins or made a 'C' shape with their hands—a reference to Vincent's childhood nickname, "Chin."

It wasn't until long after he had been caught, sentenced and had been in jail for years that the illusion he maintained finally broke. In 2003, Gigante admitted to a judge that he had been lying. He didn't come out and say *that*, of course, but the guilty plea to obstruction of justice essentially equated to, "Yes, I've been lying to you this entire time, you fools." It added a scant three years onto his sentence and allowed him to avoid the harder questions which he had tried so hard and for so long to avoid—questions pertaining to his having been the head of one of New York City's most famous and long-running Italian crime families, the Genovese.[xxiv]

VILLAGE TANNERY
173 Bleecker Street

It all started in a pizzeria at about 9:20pm on March 14th, 2007, at DeMarco's on West Houston and MacDougal Streets. It was a warm night. David had been kicked out of the place before. He was forty-two, an ex-Marine, with a history of instability and aggression. Today, he dressed carefully in a hooded sweatshirt and an obviously false grey beard, spirit-gummed to his face.

It's not clear why he decided to execute the bartender—maybe it had to do with some perceived slight, or perhaps a friend of his who had been fired from the place. At any rate, Alfredo Romero, from Puebla, Mexico, recognized Garvin behind his fake beard and icy glare. He was understandably freaked out.

The last moment of his life Romero spent handing his killer a menu with shaking hands. Once his back was turned, David Robert Garvin pulled one of the two handguns he brought with him (along with more than a hundred total rounds of ammunition) and fired fifteen shots, striking Romero twelve times. Chaos. Romero went down. Garvin walked out and stripped off his disguise, heading north. Police in a passing patrol car heard the gunfire and immediately put out a radio call. Hearing the suspect's description on the radio, two Auxiliary Officers confronted Garvin, his face still sticky with gum from the beard. He punched one of them. His gun was empty and the other was in his bag. Auxiliary Officers are civilian volunteers who, unarmed but uniformed, assist with observation and reporting duties. In this case, they followed Garvin too closely. Ahead, regular uniformed police blocked off the street in front of Garvin. Enraged and feeling trapped, he turned around. With a reloaded gun, he systematically hunted down and shot both APO Nicholas Pekearo and APO Eugene Marshalik to death outside of 209 and 208 Sullivan Street, respectively.

Drawing closer, police quickly barricaded the suspect inside the Village Tannery, a high-end West Village leather goods shop. After a brief exchange of gunfire, Garvin emerged, gun raised, and was shot to death outside of 175 Bleecker Street at about 9:30pm.[xxv]

Both the Auxiliary Officers killed in the shootout were buried with full honors and have had their names recorded at the Police Memorial.

LITTLE ITALY

Petrosino Square

Intersection of Kenmare St, Lafayette St. and Cleveland Place.

This square is named after a man who tirelessly battled crime and corruption, and is celebrated today as one of the best policemen of early New York City. He was betrayed and killed.

When you're coming across the Williamsburg Bridge into Manhattan, you'll eventually come to this tiny 'vest-pocket' park, at the intersection of Kenmare Street, Lafayette Street and Cleveland Place. Petrosino Square was originally called Kenmare Square, from 1911 until 1987. Its previous name honored the Irish birthplace of 19th-Century Lower East Side political leader "Big Tim" Sullivan's mother. In 1987, during the height of the War on Organized Crime, Kenmare Square was renamed Petrosino Square in honor of Lt. Joseph Petrosino. To this day he remains the only NYPD officer slain in the line of duty on foreign soil.

Petrosino was born in 1860 in the town of Padula, near Salerno, Italy. He immigrated to the United States at an early age and was adopted by an Irish judge after he was tragically orphaned. He was appointed to the New York City Police Department in 1883, and was the shortest officer on the force at less than five feet, four inches. Because he had knowledge of Italian dialects (which are each different enough from basic Italian to be inscrutable to many Italians, much less Americans studying Italian) he was able to infiltrate the "Black Hand," a ruthless criminal syndicate which was the forerunner of the modern Mafia.[xxvi] His investigations led him to Palermo—his mission was to obtain more information about *Mafiosi* who had infiltrated New York City, on behalf of the Department. Because administrative incompetence tipped off the press to his mission, his 'secret trip' was front-page news only days before his departure. He was legally unable to carry a firearm to defend himself while abroad, but (wrongly) believed that the gangsters would behave as they did in New York, and bring no harm to policemen. While waiting for an informant to arrive to a meeting in Palermo, he was ambushed by gunmen and shot to death. So died one of the Department's best officers.[xxvii]

IKE SEZ

If you want to visit a really interesting shop just off Broadway, visit the Evolution **Store**.

This is New York City, and it's been said that you can buy anything here, well, this store lives up to that promise, if what you want to buy is a human skeleton. Easily one of the most fascinating stores in the area, they have everything unusual: framed insects, minerals, animal skins, animal skulls and rare and exotic jewelry. Of course, they also have a children's section with games, puzzles and toys.

Old St. Patrick's

263 Mulberry Street, New York NY

Old Saint Patrick's Cathedral was defended with muskets and stones torn from the streets from people who tried to burn it down in 1836. A woman named Maria Monk wrote a book that year called "Awful Disclosures of the Hotel Dieu Nunnery of Montreal," alleging horrific abuse by some of the Catholic priests against her and others. An anti-Catholic group called the Nativists, always looking for a way to stop their religious rivals from spreading their faith, incited a riot. Although the book's accounts of horror were eventually all debunked as fake, the sensationalist work still drew enough heat to provide a case for war for the Nativists. They showed up in force, armed with clubs, hatchets, shovels, and a few firearms. The faithful, given advance warning of the attack, tore holes in the new walls that surrounded the cemetery and fortified their position. They tore out stones from the streets and hauled them up in baskets all along the Bowery, and lined along Prince Street. The column of attackers saw the ripped-up streets and knew that the "military-like" preparations were too much for their forces. They withdrew, and Old Saint Patrick's was saved.[xxviii]

This is one of the oldest churches in New York City. It was New York City's first Catholic Cathedral— its cornerstone was laid June 1809 at 263 Mulberry Street in SoHo. Although most people think of 'New' Saint Patrick's (the cathedral on Fifth Avenue between 50th and 51st Streets) when the name is spoken, 'Old' Saint Patrick's is a place of just as much beauty and historical significance.

There is something truly amazing about entering any place of worship regardless of religion; you enter and suddenly you lower your voice, your eyes are drawn upward, and, for just a moment, you're lost in the mystery and majesty of the place. Such is the case here.

Movies and Television:

This was a filming location for both "The Godfather" and "The Godfather III.[xxixxxx]" While watching "The Godfather," pay special attention to the christening scene. Something look familiar? You'll recognize the soaring interior pillars and light fixtures. The exterior shots of the scene were filmed at a different church, however.

In "The Godfather III," look for the mural behind the altar: it's in the scene where Michael Corleone is receiving a medal from the bishop in recognition of all his works on behalf of the Catholic Church.

What's Interesting?

Director Martin Scorsese lived in the area and served as an altar boy at St. Patrick's. He said that he was inspired to make the movie "Gangs of New York" after reading the Herbert Asbury book. One of Martin Scorsese early (And great films) "Mean Streets" 1973 was also filmed here.

The cemetery holds the remains of two congressmen, a naval officer, a missionary and

Pierre Toussaint; who was born into slavery in what was then the French colony of Haiti. He was brought to Manhattan by his wealthy owners. When his was freed, he started businesses and became quite successful. He used his wealth to buy others out of slavery, including his sister and the woman who would later become his wife. The Catholic Church in 1996 declared Pierre Toussaint "Venerable" by Pope John Paul II, the second step in the process of being designated a Saint in the Catholic Church. His remains were located and re-interred in what is now Saint Patrick's Cathedral, at 49th Street and Fifth Ave.

Ike Sez:

Old Saint Patrick's is a working and active parish: If you visit the church please be aware that there might be services going on. Recently Alec Baldwin of all people was married in this church.

Ravenite Social Club

247 Mulberry Street

This is a place where murders were plotted. It's also a place where one of the biggest figures in American organized crime was taken down for the last time. Nowadays, you can buy a decent pair of shoes here.

Aniello Dellacroce was a Mafia underboss and killer who sometimes dressed as a priest to confuse law enforcement. In his prime, he used 247 Mulberry—the Ravenite Social Club-- as a base of operations. After Dellacroce died on December 2nd, 1985, John Gotti knew there was no one keeping him from leadership of the Gambino crime family. No one, that is, except Paul Castellano. After Gotti had Castellano murdered at Sparks Steak House on December 16th, he moved his weekday base of operations to Dellacroce's old hideout at the Ravenite. Was it nostalgia? Bravado? Foolishness? Gotti knew the heat was getting closer, that the FBI was keeping his every move under surveillance. The Bureau tried to install listening devices in the Ravenite more than once. They knew they had to get solid wire evidence if they were going to bring the Gambinos down.[xxxi]

Mike Cirelli, Gotti's associate, was an old man in the mid-1980s. He took care of the club for years and lived above it with his wife in apartment #10. He was a tough old bird; in 1979, he chased after FBI agents with a baseball bat after they drugged the club's guard dog with sedative-laced meatballs and infiltrated the building.[xxxii] Shortly after Cirelli died in mid-January, 1988, the FBI was able to ascertain that his widow was out of the house and they got in and bugged the place. Always cagey, Gotti found an electronic listening device in the club (which wasn't effective anyway, due to both poor positioning and the near-constant din of background noise), but still missed those installed in Cirelli's old apartment. It was right here that he and his associates were recorded in high-level talks about murders and circumventing police investigations. The evidence collected from those units led to Gotti's final arrest on December 11th, 1990. He spent the rest of his life in prison until he died of cancer in 2002.

If you've ever watched those grainy black-and-white surveillance videos of John Gotti and Sammy "The Bull" Gravano walking down Mulberry Street, it is this location that is being filmed.

Now the Ravenite is a shoe store called "Shoe." Go figure.

Old Police Headquarters
240 Centre Street between Grand and Broome Streets in Little Italy

Mayor George B. McClellan commissioned a team of master architects and builders from Hoppin & Koen and Franklin B. Huntington to create this Renaissance Revival masterpiece in 1905, completed in 1909. It replaced the previous NYPD HQ at 300 Mulberry Street. The old HQ on Mulberry has since been completely torn down—there's nothing there now, except an underground parking garage and a Subway sandwich shop. 240 Centre Street was more fortunate: it was the Headquarters of the New York City Police Department until a new police headquarters was completed in 1973 by then-Mayor John V. Lindsay.

The site has been designated as a New York City landmark. The old Police Headquarters is also a filming location. If you watch old police dramas, especially the "Naked City" series from the 1950's, you will see this building while it was still the Headquarters of the New York City Police Department. On the corner of Grand Street and Center Market place is Onieals Grand Street Bar, a filming location for "Sex in the City."

IKE SEZ:

There's reportedly a secret tunnel built between the old Police Headquarters and Onieal's Tavern. The tunnel still exists, but it's now used as a wine cellar. In more recent news, 240 Centre has been converted into luxury condos for multimillionaires. All I can say is, I'm not surprised. If you can afford it, I imagine it's a nice place to live.

What's Historical?

Directly across the street from Police headquarters, #6 Centre Market Place was once the residence of photographer and photojournalist: Arthur Fellig. You may not be familiar with the name but you may know "Weegee" his nickname. During the 1930's and 40's his photos of crime scenes were published in any number of New York City newspapers. He earned the nickname "Weegee" apparently from Detectives who found him at crime scenes even before they got there. "Hey Arthur, how did you get here so fast? What? You got a Ouija board at home?" hence the nickname.

Disappearance of Etan Patz
Corner of Wooster and Prince Street

I like telling stories. But not every story has a happy ending or even an ending at all.

This one is old news, and the worst kind—the case is reopened, but word everywhere is that the reported perpetrator, one Pedro Hernandez, is about as reliable as the "what's the frequency, Kenneth?" guy who assaulted Dan Rather. Hernandez has been charged with the murder, but has a history of mental illness and hallucinations. The FBI is skeptical. That said, the NYPD's happy to be able to charge him with second degree murder for the crime to which he's confessing.[xxxiii] So:

On this bricked corner on a busy street in SoHo, little Etan Patz put on his bright blue sailor's hat and walked to the school bus for the first time. It was his last. This was over thirty years ago, before surveillance cameras were any good, before camera-phones. It was the morning of May 25, 1979—a few hours before nearly three hundred people died in Chicago when American Flight 191 crashed shortly after takeoff—but this is another story for another time…Etan. He was six, a kind-faced little boy. Soho back then was a little like parts of Brooklyn today—in '79 it was more like Bushwick is now than the gentrified ville of designer outlets and banks, of luxury lofts and celebrity restaurants.

Etan. The name reverberates. The boy has been declared dead, but the truth is that no one knows for certain what happened to him. Having a child taken is every parent's worst nightmare, without a doubt. Even a hard-hearted man wouldn't wish it on anyone.

The person who took him is officially unknown as of this writing, although two names circulate. One of them has confessed to the crime of killing Etan—that's Hernandez, the winner above. And then there's Ramos. Jose Ramos. The guy's still doing time now, finishing up a two decade sentence in Pennsylvania for molesting children. Jose Antonio Ramos. Every year, twice a year, Etan's dad sends him a poster of his boy's face. Ramos just turned sixty-seven. Etan Patz will forever be six.

The DA has reopened the case, years after the boy has been declared dead.[xxxiv] Ramos was released in November 2012, only to be immediately arrested on a Megan's Law violation. He might be out now, depending on when you're reading this. Food for thought. I suppose we'll let the boys do their work, and see what they come up with.

Umberto's Clam House (Old Location)

Corner of Mulberry and Hester Streets

The last show he ever saw was Don Rickles at the Copacabana on 60th Street, on April 6th, 1972. Joe Gallo had been known after his brief hospitalization for schizophrenia in his youth as that "little guy with balls of steel." By the time he turned forty-three, on the last night of his life, he wasn't a little guy any more. Originally born in Red Hook, Brooklyn, he rose from obscurity to become a mob boss. After hours, at about 4:30am on April 7th, Joseph and his wife Sina Essary, his daughter Lisa, his sister Carmella, and his hatchet-man "Pete the Greek" (and Pete's lady friend) sat down to eat.

His guard was down because there was an unwritten rule that Little Italy was off limits to bloodshed. It wasn't.

Somebody saw him go into Umberto's, and within minutes gunmen stormed in and shot him five times. He died at the scene. A retaliation hit in Midtown by his supporters went very wrong, but that's another story for another time.[xxxv]

IKE SEZ:

Earlier that day, Joey Gallo had visited one of his actor friends, a young fella by the name of Jerry Orbach. Jerry Orbach was working on a movie called "The Gang That Couldn't Shoot Straight" written by Jimmy Breslin. Along with appearing in this movie about an inept Brooklyn gang, Jerry Orbach also starred in a very early episode of "Kojack", where he portrayed an Assistant United States Attorney. What's also interesting is that those scenes were filmed at One Police Plaza.

Il Buco

47 Bond Street

Local legend has it that here, at 47 Bond Street, Edgar Allan Poe sat and wrote one of his best stories, *The Cask of Amontillado*. For those of you who aren't familiar with the tale, it has to do with a man burying his alcoholic friend alive inside a wall and laughing at him while he is chained there. Classic Poe. This story was first published in November 1846 in the magazine *Godey's Lady's Book*.

Nowadays, 47 Bond is an excellent classic Northern Italian restaurant, Il Buco. The prices are reasonable and the fare is great. Never forget that Poe supposedly sat in this brick-lined basement, however. Some say he haunts their wine.

But the likelihood that this story is true is almost nil; *Amontillado* is widely thought by Poe scholars to be based on his public feud with fellow literati Thomas Dunn English and Hiram Fuller, and is almost certainly not the product of a visit to a less than memorable basement.

IKE SEZ:

If Poe did have any connection to 47 Bond Street, it was through his friend Marie Louise Shew, who resided there, and whom he visited on at least one occasion. He may have written the poem *The Bells* here.

Harvey Burdell Murder

31 Bond St.

Harvey Burdell was a dentist who lived in a town house at 31 Bond Street when his landlady, a gold-digging widow named Emma Cunningham, decided she was going to marry him. He was, at least financially, a stable, secure guy -- who wouldn't want that? The fact that Burdell was a total womanizer and reputedly traded dental work for sex didn't faze her. She wanted a husband and made her intentions known. But Burdell wasn't about to buy the cow. From all accounts he liked his life just fine the way it was.

Well -- on January 30th, 1857, screams were heard coming from Burdell's office. No one bothered to investigate and the next morning his hired boy arrived at work to find the dentist dead in his own chair, strangled and stabbed and covered in blood.

A sensational trial ensued, naturally. Evidence piled up against Cunningham -- forensics suggested the killer was left-handed, for instance, and she was also left-handed -- but her lawyers used the "weaker-sex" defense and said no woman ever could've committed such a horrible, bloody crime.

It looked like Cunningham was going to get away with it. She was even able to produce a phony marriage certificate proven she and Burdell had secretly been married before his death, and it looked like she'd be able to cash in some insurance money with it. Though she spent some time in the Tombs while awaiting trial, she was ultimately acquitted.

But she got greedy.

After getting out of jail, Cunningham tried to fake a pregnancy to get even more cash out of the settlement and even went so far as to approach a doctor and ask for a baby she could pretend was hers. In a soap-worthy set up, she even *staged a fake delivery*, screaming behind a closed door for the benefit of the neighbors. But the doctor sold her out. He "delivered" her ... right into the hands of the police!

Cunningham was charged with fraud, her marriage claim to Burdell was invalidated, and she died in poverty and alone. And now? Now she is buried in the cheap seats in Green-Wood, in an impossible-to-find grave in a public lot, next to a bus station.

Less than a half-mile away, also interred in Green-Wood is her old pal, Harvey Burdell.

IKE SEZ:

You can visit both Cunningham and Burdell if you take the R train out to Brooklyn and go to Green-Wood Cemetery. The staff there will help you find their graves among the 600,000 other bodies buried in the 478-acre Victorian cemetery. It's well worth the trip to Brooklyn.

CHINATOWN

Sun Sing Theatre

75-85 E Broadway

The Sun Sing was an elaborate old theatre, once called the Florence, which served one of the dangerous neighborhoods of a New York long past. The Theatre itself was opened in 1911 as the Florence Theatre, operated by the M & S Chain. It served audiences full, sassy helpings of Yiddish vaudeville and the 1900s equivalents of blockbusters. During the 1920s, the place was packed with all kinds of shows. Just before the Second World War, the place was renovated and the seating capacity was reduced from 980 to 916. In 1942, new ownership renamed the building the New Canton Theatre, and live performances of Chinese vaudeville, opera and variety acts were put on to packed crowds.

The story behind this is that a travelling Chinese opera group was stranded in the U.S. by the war, and survived by putting on elaborate traditional shows every week for a decade. In 1950, the place was again renamed, to the Sun Sing Theatre, and the fare was changed to Chinese language films with English subtitles. The expansion of the Manhattan Bridge construction site, above, threatened the structure: it was only after heated negotiations that the building was saved. The entire neighborhood rallied to save their theatre; LIFE magazine called the Sun Sing the "only Chinese theater in America."[xxxvi] This time, the seating capacity was reduced after renovations to 676 people. The bridge now passes directly over the building.

For two decades after 1972, the Theatre offered a mixed bag of live shows and film screenings; it finally shuttered its doors for good in 1993.[xxxvii] During that time, numerous Chinese gang-related incidents of violence and shootings occurred at the site. Nowadays, the original structure is there, but what's inside is long gone. It's a Chinese variety store nowadays, with cheap ceramic knickknacks, plastic 'lucky cats' meant to bring good fortune to businesses, and a plethora of off-brand or outdated electronics.

The Sun Sing Theatre Today; Directly beneath the Manhattan Bridge.

Golden Star Bar

9 East Broadway

In 1856 outside of San Francisco, the criminal brotherhood known as the Hip Sing was born. For decades, they fought with their rivals, the On Leong Tong; for a time at the end of the 19th century, this little stretch of East Broadway was the bloodiest block in America.

Herbert Liu was never a member of the secretive Euro-American organization, the Masons. He called his gang the Chinese Freemasons because it was a symbolic gesture, a nod to history. The Freemasons in Chinese popular history were rebels against the Manchu in 19th-century China. The Ghost Shadows gang, wary of these newcomers, and acting on the orders of Benny Ong (the leader of the Hip Sing at the time), came and shot up the place on the early morning of December 23, 1982. Eleven Ghost Shadows gang members were hit; three of that number died. This shootout at the Golden Star led to the dissolution of the Freemasons. Now, the bar is closed.[xxxviii]

Chatham Square

Where Mott Street intersects with the Bowery

Many streets and many stories flow into Chatham. Chatham Square was historically a gathering place for many of the Chinese gangs that populated the area from the mid-nineteenth century onwards. According to the *Encyclopedia of International Organized Crime*, the Off-Track Betting outlet here, in the heart of NYC's Chinatown, was the city's top revenue producing OTB site for many years.

Furthermore, the American-style tattoo was born here.[xxxix] Some of the finest examples of early American classic maritime tattoos come from Chatham, especially Charlie Wagner's Black Eye Barbershop. This icon of modern skin art held court at Chatham for decades. Additionally, Samuel J. O'Reilley's modern tattoo machine was created and patented at the Black Eye.[xl]

Lastly, the new Second Avenue subway line will have a major station planned for Chatham Square.

Ah Kay's Casino

125 East Broadway:

In 1982, Ah Kay was a rising star in the Chinese gangster criminal underworld. He joined Fuk Ching ("Fook Ching"), which was short for Fukien Chingnian, or 'Fujianese Youth.' That small, tightly-knit organization was born on Grand Street, when there were not many Fujianeses in New York City. At that time, Fuk Ching was run by its founder, Kin Fei Wong (also known as "Foochow Paul"). The gang's territory has been acknowledged by many experts to be limited to Eldridge and Chrystie streets.[xli] These same experts have acknowledged that extortion of local businesses by the gang remains relatively common. During the Moon Festival (which occurs every September), groups of gang-affiliated youths go door to door, selling moon cakes for exorbitant, 'lucky' (ending in $--8) prices.

By spring of 1990, Ah Kay had become the ringleader of the Fuk Ching, and moved down to Chinatown. He decided it was time to create a new headquarters, so he established a casino and meeting-house at 125 East Broadway, and put the word out that it would open on October 1st of 1990. As predicted, the rival gangs, particularly the Tung On, took notice. A posse of Tung On youth arrived that very afternoon, demanding 'lucky money.' Ah Kay refused, saying he'd kill the gangsters. He then returned inside, but his men stayed outside. Both groups of gang members pulled pistols and fired at each other. Ah Kay's little brother was wounded and pulled to cover. Shell casings littered the pavement. The Tung Ons withdrew to safety.

This pattern of violence and intimidation between the gangs repeated itself over and over in the early 1990s. In many instances, a Fuk Ching gunman would sprint away from the police, the NYPD in hot pursuit, and would disappear into 125 East Broadway's maze of hidden rooms and secret doors. As early as 1991, a Senate subcommittee mentioned Ah Kay as the leader of Fuk Ching.[xlii]

Ah Kay ended up getting nailed by the Feds; rather than spend the rest of his days rotting in prison, he chose to cooperate. The string of prominent Chinatown gangsters whose operations were ultimately compromised by Ah Kay gave the government a new insight into the workings of these 'tongs' (worker associations, another word for Chinese mobs).

Sister Ping, Human Smuggler

47 East Broadway

47 East Broadway looks like nothing special. Perhaps, now, it *is* nothing special. After all, Sister Ping isn't there any more. Sister Ping wasn't a facilitator of destinations. Sister Ping *was* the destination. She was a one-stop traveling shop, and could get you where you needed to go quickly and, usually, safely. Border guards in some third country a problem? She knows them, or her organization does. She's already paid them off.

Cheng Chui Ping, known as Ping Jie ("Big Sister Ping" or simply "Sister Ping") was a renowned smuggler of people in the 1980s. Fujianese? No visa? Need to get to New York City in a hurry? No problem. Sister Ping would arrange for you to get there. She had people with money in China; you'd pay them, and then arrangements would be made. Her business was word of mouth, and she did very well. Although she didn't look like much—she never drove fancy cars, or wore ostentatious jewelry—Sister Ping was a veritable business magnate of the Fujianese underworld.

Although she is no longer practicing, having long since been caught and turned by the Feds, you'll be pleased to know that she associated heavily, although often involuntarily, with Ah Kay, who is mentioned previously. In fact, when Ah Kay was himself caught, he all but told the Federal agents: "I can give you Sister Ping." And he did.[xliii]

47 East Broadway Today

15 Pell St:

On Leong Tong Merchant's Association Historic HQ

The On Leong Tong ("Peaceful Dragon Parlor") has always been a kind of trade association of professionals. In every society, there are immigrants who form their own organizations and affiliations. The On Leong Tong is a kind of tradesmen's association of business owners and community leaders…at least on the outside. Inside, it has been described as a culture highly steeped in criminal lore.

In the New York City branch (there are branches of the On Leong Tong in nearly every major American city with a sizable Chinese population); the Tong is an organization which has been affiliated for years with gang activity. Before the Hip Sing Tong leader Mock Duck arrived in the city, around 1900, the On Leong Tong operated with impunity and raked in massive profits from extortion, gambling, and other lucrative ventures. Their leader, Tom Lee, was the undisputed ruler of Chinatown.

Mock Duck came with his chainmail vest and his hatchets and his pistols, and offered Lee a deal: half and half, or war. Lee chose war, and wars between the two Tongs came and went over the next years. There were two major conflicts: 1904 to 1906 and 1909 to 1913. These wars are where the term "hatchet man" (meaning muscle or lackey) comes from; the subordinates of both Tongs routinely used small axes hidden in their sleeves as close-quarters combat weapons.[xliv]

IKE SEZ:

Stand at the intersection of Doyers and Pell Street, (the corner to your right if you're standing in front of 15 Pell Street), and do a 360 degree turn. There is no more an iconic view of Chinatown as this intersection: It captures all the beauty, mystery and intrigue of this neighborhood. It is virtually unchanged in over a hundred years.

Harmony Palace

94 Mott St

Wing Yeung Chan, also known as 'Big Head,' was kind of like NYC Chinatown's Biggie Smalls. He was no lyrical genius, but worked his way up from being a dishwasher up to the head of the On Leong's Merchant's Association—that is to say, the quasi-industrial trade union known as the On Leong Tong. He was also the head of the gang known as the Ghost Shadows, who at their peak made hundreds of thousands of dollars every month from extortion, sex trafficking, contract murder and illegal narcotics. They answered to the On Leong Tong, which Chan controlled. He made his HQ this huge restaurant on Mott Street, the Harmony Palace. It could seat four hundred people, had the best dim sum in Chinatown, and much more. It was here that Chan plotted hits, issued orders to make deals and sell drugs, moved money and shipped people—all for a price.[xlv]

Chan was ultimately caught and charged with numerous federal crimes, including murder, conspiracy to traffic and distribute illegal narcotics, human trafficking, conspiracy to import illegal aliens, as well as unlawful imprisonment and sex slaves.[xlvi]

In a move that mimicked Ah Kay's earlier turnaround, Chan turned informant and helped the Federal agents dismantle the organization he so carefully created.

Now you can get some amazing food here. Go to it; life is short and the bad man is gone. Go on.

FINANCIAL CENTER

Wall Street

This is another street where blood was spilled. One of NYC's first acts of major terrorism took place here. Anarchists detonated over a hundred pounds of dynamite on a horse cart on Thursday, September 16, 1920 at exactly 12:01 PM. Today, people walk by Broad and Wall every day without knowing what happened here. But you do. In addition to the poor horse, thirty-eight people were killed and over a hundred forty-three were badly hurt.[xlvii] Coming around the front of the building on foot, find the JP Morgan Building's entrance. Just left and right of the entrance, on the wall there, run your hands along the limestone wall. Feel the blast and shrapnel scars from the explosion: they remain a haptic reminder of the city's deadly criminal past, and a lifeline to the lessons of the future.

Location: Runs West to East from Broadway, directly in front of Trinity Church on the west side to the east river; open to Pedestrian Traffic only. Take the IRT #4, 5 Train and Exit at the Wall Street Station, or take the BMT "J and Z" train and exit at Broad Street station.

What's Historical?

This street was once the barrier between civilization and mosquito-ridden swamp and brush. Back in the 1600s, this street was originally an actual wooden log wall called a palisade. It stretched from the Hudson River down to the East River. Even back then, they were afraid of Staten Island.

What's Interesting? Walk down Wall Street and stop at #40 Wall Street. What once was called the Bank of Manhattan Building is now The Trump Building, Donald Trump having purchased it in 1995. But what's interesting is that when the building was completed it was the tallest building in the world. There was a race at the time between this building, and the Chrysler building for naming rights to the tallest building in the world. 40 Wall Street won, but only briefly. Less than a month after the building was completed, the Chrysler Building has a secret spire lifted into place, making the Chrysler Building then the tallest building in the world.

What's Close-By? Walk back to Broadway and turn right, walking north about two blocks and you'll find Zucotti Park, the site of the Occupy Wall Street movement which began September 17, 2011. Mostly a very peaceful place now, it was the site of sometimes violent clashes between the NYPS and protesters.

Police Museum: Old First Police Precinct
100 Old Slip, New York NY 10005

This building was constructed between 1909 and 1911, around the same time that the NYPD headquarters moved from 300 Mulberry Street (where Teddy Roosevelt had held court until 1897 or so), to 240 Centre Street. Originally the First Precinct, 100 Old Slip remained so until 1973, when it was repurposed with a terse order from Michael J. Codd.[xlviii] It wasn't until December 2001 that the building was rededicated by Rudolf Giuliani.

The Police Museum is a necessary place, and the men and women who have served the Department over the years deserve to be remembered. Being a police officer, especially a "uniform," is a largely thankless job—there's a lot of standing around, a fair amount of politics, and an incredible amount of paperwork and waiting around for things to happen, all the while with the constant weight of all your equipment weighing down on your hips and legs and knees. This reality, however, has done little to dampen the public fascination with both sides of the law. Whether it's interesting or not (and I think it is), police are out there every day, dealing with the public. And it can be dangerous. Here, you can see a small part of what it was like to be a cop through New York City's history, and a little of what it is like now.

What's Interesting? They have a simulator which lets you pick up a wired, simulated gun and test your reflexes, wits, and good judgment in a series of situations where you (like police when things go wrong) have a split second to decide to shoot or not to shoot.

Every year the **Police Museum** a car show old police vehicles. It's great for nostalgia and car buffs alike. And it's free.

What's Close-By? This area has been recently renovated and there is a wonderful park called the East River Piers. There is plenty of room to see and watch the east river go by. Pier 11, just a block north from old slip is a launching location of any number of ferries to Brooklyn, including a ferry to IKEA Express Shuttle to Brooklyn. You can find a schedule at www.NYWATERTAXI.com

Fraunces Tavern and Museum
54 Pearl Street

New York City was briefly the seat of the American government, before it moved down to Philadelphia and then to D.C. At the end of the successful American Revolution, in 1783, General George Washington bid farewell to his officers during a banquet that was held in what's called the "Tallmadge Room" today and was called the "Long Room" back then.[xlix] One of New York's oldest buildings, Fraunces Tavern was rebuilt in 1905 to resemble the original structure. It is now owned by one of the best breweries in Ireland, Porterhouse, and houses a small museum commemorating Washington's speech, and the American Revolution itself.

Like every place in the city, blood was spilled here, too: on January 24, 1975, a bomb exploded at this site. Four people were killed, and approximately 150 were injured. The terrorist group FALN (Armed Forces for the Liberation of Puerto Rico) took credit for the attack, but to this date, the case remains unsolved.[l]

IKE SEZ:

If you're a beer drinker, try the Wrasslers Stout. It's honest, Irish, well balanced and strong. The food is excellent, too. Make reservations if you want to eat! Fraunces Tavern has now been extended to the buildings next door, creating a labyrinth of old world rooms, with original woodwork, tin ceilings, prints and fireplaces.

St. Paul's Chapel
209 Broadway, between Fulton and Vesey Street

Completed in 1766, St. Paul's Chapel is the oldest house of worship in New York City. George Washington came here to pray after being inaugurated as the first President of the United States. The Chapel has survived revolution, terrorism, pollution, legislation, riots, civil war, renovations, and the Great Fire of 1835, among many, many other things; in more recent years, it served as a refuge for first responders and those who needed solace immediately after the terrorist attacks of September 11th, 2001.

In those dark hours, New York's Bravest and Finest were on duty indefinitely. The bridges were closed. Public transit was suspended. Civilians walked in stunned, soot-covered throngs back home over the silent bridges. At St. Paul's, it was not unusual to see exhausted cops and firefighters sleeping in the pews. The dust from the debris from the explosions and fires choked the streets outside and the men and women tracked it in.[li]

Today, the Chapel has an extensive collection of artifacts that were left behind by both law enforcement and firefighting personnel who worked at the site.

Ike Sez:
The Chapel is likely one of the most spiritually moving and poignant places you will ever visit, regardless of your faith or affiliation. The sacrifice of both common New Yorkers and first responders in these uncommon times has left its indelible mark. The feeling of history is powerful here.

Police Memorial
Corner Liberty and West Street

This sheaf of black granite is down in Battery Park City. It is a solid wall inscribed with the names of those NYPD officers who have died as a result of active service, so that they may be remembered for all time for their bravery and selfless devotion to duty. There are about seven hundred names in all—Joseph Petrosino is there—as well as the names some three score of officers who died as a result of the September 11th, 2001 terrorist attacks. Also included are the names of Auxiliary Officers who have been killed in the line of duty. The Wall is for our memories of those who served. If you know anyone in the NYPD, take a moment when you're in Battery Park and pay the Memorial a visit. The sense of history there is a deep one. This monument to liberty, duty, and sacrifice is, fittingly, adjacent to the fragment of the Berlin Wall on display here in the city.

What's Historical?

Right next to the Police Memorial, a non-descript, understated slab of concrete is mounted behind a fence. It is a remnant of the Berlin Wall, the barrier between the American and Soviet zones in the divided capital of Cold War Berlin. The Wall's fall, in 1989, was a symptom of a deeper malady in the systemic inefficiency of the Soviet system. When the people finally rose up, it was after decades of gradual reform and compromise. The free flow of information and culture which resulted from these and other youth rebellions eventually led to the dissolution of the Soviet Union and the creation of the post-Cold War power structures which we see today. It remains a tangible piece of history which inspires even today, especially in the wake of the Arab Spring and other revolutions worldwide.

IKE SEZ:

The piece of the Wall is just a slab of concrete daubed with spray paint behind a spiked metal gate. It doesn't look like much, and maybe, now, it's not. I don't think so, though. I'm not much for symbolism, or metaphysics—never been much else than a literal guy. I see myself in the here and now. I do think, however, that it is significant that this monument to freedom is so close to the Police Memorial. People died to try to cross this thing that separated families, lives, careers, societies. They were shot down like animals by the Stasi and chased with dogs. Most of history's remnants are non-descript when they exist at all. This is a tangible reminder of oppression, and it speaks to higher values than survival. When I see this chunk of spray-painted concrete, I think long and hard about what it means to be an American.

CIVIC CENTER

NYS Supreme Court
60 Centre Street, New York, NY

The Supreme Court of the United States first met in New York, in 1790. The Justices originally started meeting down in the old Merchant's Exchange building, which was down on what is now Exchange Street; it burned down in the Great Fire of 1836.[lii]

The NYS Supreme Court is one of New York City's most iconic locations; it has been seen countless times in television shows. Heard of a show called "Law and Order?" The Supreme Court is on the show: if you stand at the top of the stairs between the Corinthian columns, you'll put yourself in a "Law and Order" film shot. This scene has been in countless episodes, usually at its conclusion.

"Night Court?" It's been on that one as well[liii]. The Supreme Court was also the filming location for one of the most dramatic scenes in the movie "The Godfather," where Barzini is messily shot to death on its steps of the courthouse after his release by a judge.[liv] It is also a location for the movie "Twelve Angry Men," the excellent film adaptation of the courtroom drama, featuring Henry Fonda, Lee J. Cobb and Jack Klugman.[lv]

IKE SEZ:

Many years ago was working a uniform overtime detail right in the middle of Foley Square where the Supreme Court Building stands. Who walks up to me? **Jack Klugman**. And I greet with "Hiya Jack, how are ya?" We talked for a while and then he asked me directions to the Woolworth Building. Yeah, like he really needed them from me.

What's Interesting?

Recently the New York Post discovered that he inscription above front colonnade is wrong: It turns out that it's supposed to read "The *due* administration of justice is the firmest pillar of good government". It was a quote from a letter y George Washington.

Federal Plaza, Foley Square
Broadway between Worth and Duane Streets.

The Federal Bureau of Investigation has their field office here, on the 23rd Floor; the Department of Homeland Security also maintains a presence here. With the increasing rapidity of information transfer and the explosive growth of technology, it is necessary for the Federal Government to maintain a powerful presence in American metropolitan centers. Globalization has brought us many things—clean water to billions, advanced wireless networks connecting isolated rural communities to the rest of the world, and incredible leaps and bounds in other technologies.

However, the rate of political, social and economic change has only increased as well. To keep up, the Bureau's dedication to safety and preparedness in our communities has achieved a new height in the twenty-first century. I've worked on cases where they were involved, mostly having to do with organized crime. I can say that the men and women, both agents and analysts, work very hard and take their jobs extremely seriously. This was true before 9/11, and it's doubly true today. In my opinion, the NYPD has made the right move by cross training with these and other organizations, as well as engaging in an increasing level of information-sharing and community outreach.

They're busy; don't go in there and bother them (I know you wouldn't), but by all means give them a call if you have a problem. They're at (212) 384-1000.

IKE SEZ:

26 Federal Plaza stands on what was once the Collect Pond; once a main source for fresh water in what was the New Amsterdam. It was fed by a stream that ran under what is now Canal Street to the north. Large private homes once stood just north of the pond. Many years later, the pond became the source for water for what was then known as "The Old Brewery"; part of the Five Points. The New York State Supreme Court now stands on that spot.

"The Tombs" and Night Court

100 Center Street. New York NY

"The Tombs" is the longstanding name for the lockup, mainly for minor offenses. It looks from the outside like a tremendous grey monolith—windows are few, if any. Prisoners are greeted with a whiff of pungent Chinatown air from the cracked-open front windows of the squad car or police van that transports them here; they come down into a secure garage and then they're escorted inside. They're searched and run through a metal detector. All is dark and quiet but for the rumbling of vehicles and the light slap of your own feet on the tile. Buzzing fluorescent lights, desolate. Walls with cracks as thick as your fingers. A rattling of chains.

There's an initial processing; everywhere there are police personnel, and the reek of unwashed people, the crazies, and people who sit quietly. Once you're in, they maybe feed you once or twice a night—a carton of milk, a bologna sandwich on white bread. You're put in a large cell with twenty or thirty other people of the same sex. No one's happy about being there—some of them talk. Most of the real baddies have been transported elsewhere; 100 Centre is a holding place, a place of transition. It is where people who want to cross the river wait if they lack the proverbial two pieces of silver. Most of them take their shoes off and use them as a pillow under their heads to sleep if they can—a sweatshirt is bundled over them and draped over the eyes.

Or people smoke: folks who've been locked up before are fast and savvy when it comes to breaking up cigarettes into their pockets and grinding the tobacco down into them while they're being arrested, transported or processed. Matches are hidden and carefully cut into pieces lengthwise later—striking strips are concealed as well, torn from matchbooks. Any kind of paper can be tumbled soft enough to smoke if it's broken down first, rolled between the palms vigorously. There's little to nothing else to do in jail—everyone is just waiting to get out. It is a place of calm desperation, tinged with sadness.

1 Hogan Place- the New York District Attorney's Office; Peter Gripaldi Shooting and Indictment

Every now and then, astute observers can point to a certain crime or incident as being the harbinger of things to come.

This story is about Russian crime organizations taking hold in New York City back in the Clinton administration. It's also basically about a man getting shot in the crotch.

The New York District Attorney is generally regarded as the top prosecutor of the State. In the early 1990s, they were busier than ever; the city was undergoing a critical reaction to the crack epidemic, and tensions were higher than ever. The War on Crime was beginning to show chinks in its armor.

But this story isn't about the New York District Attorney. It's about a case they handled. It's about a silencer, about a scam, about a hit man. Lastly, of course, it's about model trains.

Michael Lipkin had been a stockbroker before he gave it up. Well, *gave it up* isn't the right phrase: he lost his license as part of a settlement with the Attorney General. He agreed to the settlement, his attorney says, because he was already out of the securities and exchange business. He had nothing to lose. The settlement was for the Mugs Plus scam.

According to documents filed in the New York Supreme Court, it went like this: some Russian scam artists (headed by one Vadim Kaplun, an unlicensed stockbroker) sold phony stock for a company based in New Jersey, called Mugs Plus. Unknown to would-be investors, Mugs Plus didn't even have a working factory. The stock was a sham, and the company produced nothing. The scammers would then funnel money into their bank accounts; most of the $1 million dollars was withdrawn in cash.

In early June 1993, someone wanted something to happen to Lipkin. It seems likely, looking at the facts, that this wasn't a planned assassination. If Gripaldi had wanted Lipkin dead, he had ample opportunity to kill him. Peter Gripaldi had flown into NYC some days earlier from California. He was a hit man by reputation who had done work for various criminal organizations in the past. When he arrived at Lipkin's office, the two men had a brief conversation. Then Gripaldi pulled out a silenced, fully automatic machine pistol and shot Lipkin in the crotch and, after a short struggle, walked out the door. Lipkin, bleeding everywhere, chased Gripaldi outside and shot and wounded his assailant with his own gun.

Gripaldi was convicted of this shooting by the D.A.; he is now in prison and spends his time building model trains. Lipkin later was indicted in New Jersey for his participation in a fuel scam in that state.[lvi]

One Police Plaza

Commissioned by then-Mayor John Lindsay and completed in 1973, this 13-story building on Park Row remains to this day the Headquarters of the New York City Police Department.[lvii] On the eighth floor, NYPD technicians staff the RTCC (Real-Time Crime Center), one of the most advanced domestic computer networks in the United States.

Utilizing data aggregation programs, the system pulls data by the minute and puts the pieces together using predictive algorithms to help police officers determine where to put more boots on the street, and when.

Additionally, the system allows near immediate cross-referencing of investigative resources, such as suspect dossiers or distinguishing characteristics.[lviii] This place, as you might infer, is heavily guarded at all hours of the day. The large red sculpture that you see as you walk toward the main entrance is called "5 in 1" by the late Tony Rosenthal, who died in July, 2009. The piece is intended to represent the five boroughs of New York City.

On "Law & Order: Criminal Intent," there's an extended shot at the end of the first episode of each season which shows the protagonists walking outside the building.[lix] Previously, the NYPD had its headquarters on Centre Street between Broome and Grand, near "The Tombs" at 100 Centre. "The Tombs" is the lockup; you don't want to go there.

The pedestrian walkway leading up to the main entrance is also a filming location; on several occasions while going in and out of the building it wasn't unusual to see "Law & Order" actors Jerry Orbach, Sam Waterston and Benjamin Bratt standing around waiting to set up a shot.

What's Interesting?

One Police Plaza stands on the spot of what once was the Sugar House Prison during the revolutionary war in America. A remnant of that prison, a window with Iron Bars in embedded into a wall between the Municipal Building and grounds of One Police Plaza.

Ike Sez

After you leave One Police Plaza, walk south toward the Brooklyn Bridge. There is a pedestrian plaza which leads you to the pedestrian walkway over the Brooklyn Bridge. I recommend a walk across the Brooklyn Bridge because the views are incredible, and it cost nothing. The main span is only about 1600 feet, but the views of lower Manhattan are incredible, and it costs nothing to do.

African Burial Ground

Everywhere beneath us in New York City, there lie the dead. They are all through the soil and the streets—their bones are everywhere. The city wasn't always so big, of course—what's now a large chunk of the northern Financial District used to be wild lands outside the boundaries of the Dutch palisades. People were mainly buried in what's now the cemetery of Trinity Church in those early years in the mid-seventeenth century.

Slavery, regrettably, was also a fact of life in those days. There was human trafficking in New Amsterdam (the Dutch name for New York) almost from the start. They came in 1626, brought by the seventeenth century's version of a megacorporation: the Dutch West India Company. These people were brought mainly from West and Central Africa to work as slaves—they and their descendents worked for more than two hundred years in New York City, until slavery was finally outlawed in June 1827. More than ten thousand slaves were buried on what was then the outskirts of the city.

In 1991 and 1992, excavation for a new Federal Building at 290 Broadway unearthed scores of long-forgotten human remains. Work on the structure was halted, and the Federal Government declared the grounds a National Historic Landmark a year later. The plans for the Federal Building were adjusted to build around it once the sensitive legal and political issues were sorted out; in 2003 (the proceedings were substantially delayed by the terror attacks of September 11th, 2001). Although only a tiny fraction (perhaps four hundred or so out of a suspected fifteen thousand or more) of the total bodies buried in the Burial Ground were recovered during the excavation process for the Federal Building, they have been the subject of intense scrutiny by researchers. Ethnographic studies have focused on everything from the diet of the decedents, to jewelry, to signs of tuberculosis and other diseases. The African Burial Ground Museum is a lasting tribute to the ingenuity, resilience, and steadfastness of spirit of some of New York City's oldest residents.[lx]

Bernie Goetz

Chambers Street IRT #1, 2, 3 Subway Station; Corner of Chambers Street and West Broadway.

Bernie Goetz was a nice guy. The city—it used to not be so nice. Especially the subway. Go down there now—it's rare to see graffiti. Say what you will about the fare hikes; I'll take a clean subway car any day. But this story isn't about graffiti. And maybe Bernie wasn't so nice. Maybe he was tired of being nice. NYC in the 80s and early 90s was a dangerous place.

Maybe Bernie was scared. Maybe he was tired of being pushed around. What we know is this: he brought an illegal handgun with him on the 2 train. Four men, Daryl Caby, James Ramseur, Barry Allen, and Troy Canty approached him just south of 14th Street and asked for five dollars. The men say they were panhandling; Goetz says he feared for his life. He shot all four men within one and three-quarters seconds, missing one shot and attempting to shoot Canty again. Canty would never walk again; the other men were hospitalized and injured.

Immediately after the shooting stopped, Goetz checked to make sure he didn't hit the two women cowering in the train (everyone else had fled), and then the conductor appeared, asking if he was a cop. He said no (truthfully) and refused to hand over his weapon, instead running onto the train tracks and exiting the system here, at Chambers. He then went on the run for a few days before turning himself in, becoming the center of a firestorm of controversy.[lxi] Even today, after the city's safety record is one of the best in the world, Goetz is still famous as a vigilante. One of the men Goetz shot, James Ramseur, recently passed on. After being shot by Goetz, he did hard time for sexually assaulting a pregnant woman with a pistol.

IKE SEZ:

By chance, I knew Mr. Goetz personally before the shootings occurred. In 1979, I was working as an assistant manager trainee at a Gristede's Supermarket on 14th Street. Mr. Goetz lived down the block at 55 West 14th Street. He often shopped at the store, and it was my responsibility to "okay" his paying by personal check. I read his name and told him that my name was unusual, too. Interestingly, he was one of the quietest, meekest, most unassuming people I have ever met. Immediately after the shooting, my lovely wife saw the "wanted" poster and recognized him. Several days later, Bernhard Hugo Goetz turned himself in at a police station in New Hampshire.

I'm glad I always Okayed his checks.

Bernie Goetz's' Residence at the time of the incident: 55 West 14th Street:

Murder of James Davis

City Hall

It was a hot day in the City Council when Othniel Askew murdered Councilman Davis. James Davis was well liked in his district. An ex-cop, Davis was a tall, hearty, take-charge kind of man who was able to bring people together. He brought people over to his side, most particularly in Crown Heights. In the heady days of the 1990s, it seemed like anything could happen.

It nearly did—in 1991, a member of Crown Heights' Jewish Lubavitch sect struck and killed the child of Guyanese immigrant, bringing simmering racial tensions in the neighborhood to an explosion. The Crown Heights riots of 1991 were the result.

A former corrections officer, police officer, and a minister, Davis eventually got his chance and became a leader, with a message of peace. He got a seat in Brooklyn's 35th District as a Councilman, and from there began bringing communities together in nonviolence around him. It was Davis who helped bring the feuding communities together in marches for peace and nonviolence. His message was a simple and compelling one.

Othniel Askew was a political rival of Davis, though not a serious one. He had walked into Davis' life only two weeks earlier, and had quickly become dangerously obsessed with the man.[lxii] He was concerned about a lot of things—that people would find out he was gay and HIV-positive, that he wouldn't beat Davis in the election coming up, and more. He was about a decade younger than Davis and a bit more aggressive in his was a former police officer and was likely armed in the Council chambers. In the weeks before the incident he had been acting more and more erratically, making wild allegations and claims.

Hours before he walked into the Council chambers with Davis, Othniel Askew had gone to the FBI. He claimed he was being blackmailed, and that Councilman Davis had offered him a no-show job, a building in Brooklyn, and a $45,000 bribe. After he was done with that, Askew left his last will and testament on a table at his home. In his pockets he brought an unsigned letter, purportedly from Davis, thanking him for his support, another document outlining his duties as an aide to Davis, and a loaded .40 caliber pistol. In his sock he put four extra bullets.

It was the courtesy extended to all councilmembers and their guests that they be escorted around the metal detector. Askew knew this, and he knew he wanted the councilman dead, no matter the cost. He brought a .40 caliber automatic pistol with him that day and four extra rounds in his sock. Davis introduced Askew to one of his colleagues, and then moments later Askew shot Davis twice in the chest. Moments later, the killer was fatally shot by a member of Davis' security detail.[lxiii] Mayor Bloomberg immediately changed the rules about the metal detectors.[lxiv]

First Police Precinct

16 Ericsson Place, New York, NY, 10013

The First Precinct was originally located at 100 Old Slip (now the Police Museum). It was relocated by the orders of Chief Inspector Cobb in 1973.[lxv] Today, it is an administrative hub only secondary to the New York Police Department Headquarters in importance.

The First Precinct retained formal "case responsibility" for the World Trade Center Attacks, and its detectives and investigators were instrumental in both the first response as well as with providing assistance to the various Federal agencies which helped coordinate the initial actions and massive cleanup effort after the attacks.

Today, its officers and detectives protect the heart of TriBeCa and its environs (including the NYC streets leading to the Holland Tunnel) from threats. This neighborhood was once called home by both John F. Kennedy Jr, at 20 North Moore Street, and the late actor Heath Ledger, at 421 Broome Street.

What's Interesting?

Just across the street from the First Precinct is the New York City Fire Department Hook and Ladder#8 which was used as a filming location as the headquarters for the **"Ghostbusters"** Movie (1984). When you stop by take a peek inside: On the left side wall you can still see the "Ghostbusters" sign.

US Customs House
One Bowling Green

Back in the early period of our nation's history, customs and excise taxes were the primary source of income for the Federal Government—America's infamous income tax laws weren't passed until 1918. These first income-producing edicts were what pulled our indebted nation (the Revolution had been expensive) out of insolvency in those first few uncertain years.[lxvi]

This building was finished in 1907, and located on the spot where Fort Amsterdam once stood, its palisades keeping the fledgling city secure. Just outside the fort, the first recorded killing in what would become New York was committed on September 6th, 1609.[lxvii] John Colman, an English sailor aboard the Dutch ship the *Half Moon*, was reportedly slain by Native Americans in a skirmish after a reconnaissance party Colman led was ambushed. The best records available indicate he was hit in the throat with a stone-tipped arrow.[lxviii] The facts remain hazy, not least because the killing is now over four hundred years old.

The U.S. Customs house now houses the National Museum of the American Indian, and the beautiful arches and sweeping interior lines of the structure give the incisive, intelligent exhibits of the museum the perfect home.

What's Interesting?

The U.S. Customs house now houses the National Museum of the American Indian, and the beautiful arches and sweeping interior lines of the structure give the incisive, intelligent exhibits of the museum the perfect home. This museum is part of the Smithsonian Museum.

The Museum is situated across from Bowling Green Park, New York City's Oldest Park. The park served as the council ground for Native American tribes. Ironically it is also the site where Peter Minuit purchased Manhattan Island from the Native Americans. This spot also marks the start of Broadway, and it is from here that the famous New York City Ticker Tape parades start, honoring everyone from the Apollo 11 astronauts to the New York Yankees. But walk north on Broadway and watch your step; as you walk, you will find embedded into the sidewalk a timeline of these ticker tape parades and who was honored.

Ike Sez: Just north of Bowling Green Park is the famous Wall Street Bull. Incredibly there are days when you have to wait in line to get your picture taken with the bull. Most people take a picture in front of the bull, that is, on the north side, but you would be amazed to see how many take a picture of the south, or backside of the bull.

Staten Island Ferry
South Ferry

The Ferry is one of the best-kept little secrets of New York. It's *free*, gives you a taste of the fresh air and the sea, and makes for a great date. They serve beer and so on downstairs. The best time to go is around August or September, just before sunset: you get postcard views of Ellis Island, Governors' Island and Liberty Island, home to the Statue of Liberty. If you do happen to be on a date right now, poke that person and ask to go. It's worth it, and I mean it when I say it's free. It's the best way to get to Staten Island if you have the time—the actual best way to get to Staten is by driving across the Verrazano Bridge, but then you have to worry about parking. And we all know what that's like.

Staten Island is quirky and fun. It's like Times Square: most New Yorkers avoid it like the plague. You'll gain instant street cred with any real New Yorker if you tell them that you went down there. The people who live down there swear by it. What does Ike like? Ike likes Queens, but that's just Ike.

So go down to Staten on the Ferry when the weather's nice. Make a day of it. Just don't get lost; you may end up living there. That's how they get you.

Like every place in the city, the Ferry is no stranger to tragedy: on October 15th, 2003, the ferry *Andrew J. Barberi* crashed into a pier on the Staten Island Side, killing eleven people.[lxix] On July 7th, 1986, a deranged 43-year old Cuban émigré, Juan J. Gonzalez, stabbed and killed two people and wounded nine others with a two-foot ornamental sword he bought in Times Square. He was stopped by a retired

police officer who, fortunately for most of the passengers aboard, was carrying his .38 with him.[lxx]
Goes to show: this is a safe city, but watch your back.

The Ferry is down on the southernmost tip of Manhattan Island, and runs 24 hours a day.

IKE SEZ:

When you board the ferry on the Manhattan side, walk to the other end of the ferry where you will have a great view of the Statue of Liberty. On the way back from Staten Island, again, walk to the other end of the ferry and get your camera ready for postcard-perfect photos of the Lower Manhattan skyline.

---

[i] Edward T O'Donnell, *Ship ablaze: the tragedy of the steamboat General Slocum*, (New York City: Broadway Books, 2003).
[ii] Eric Ferrara, *Gangsters, Murderers and Weirdos of the Lower East Side, Part 1* , (New York City: Lulu.com, 2008), p.34.
[iii] Metro US, "Money from drug bust now helping Bronx teens." Last modified January 18, 2012. http://www.metro.us/newyork/local/article/1074842--money-from-drug-bust-now-helping-bronx-teens.
[iv] David, Larry, & Seinfeld, Jerry, "Seinfeld," 1989-1998, Television.
[v] Eric Ferrara, *Gangsters, Murderers and Weirdos of the Lower East Side, Part 1* , (New York City: Lulu.com, 2008), p.31.
[vi] Jack Henry Abbott, *In the belly of the beast: letters from prison*, (New York City: Vintage Books, 1991).
[vii] David K Frasier, *Murder cases of the twentieth century: biographies and bibliographies of 280 convicted or accused killers*, (Jefferson, NC: McFarland & Co, 1996).
[viii] USA Today, "Murderer Jack Henry Abbott commits suicide." Last modified February 10, 2002. Accessed May 2, 2012.
http://www.usatoday.com/news/nation/2002/02/10/abbott.htm.
[ix] Al Silverman, *Foster and Laurie*, (New York City: Little, Brown & Co, 1974).
[x] IIall, Vondie Curtis, "Glitter," 2001, Film.
[xi] Bochco, Steven, & Milch, David, "NYPD Blue," 1993-2005, Television.
[xii] Marlowe, Andrew W, "Castle," 2009-, Television.
[xiii] Mann, Abby, "Kojak," 1973-1978, Television.

[xiv] Avedon, Barbara, & Corday, Barbara, "Cagney and Lacey," 1982-1988, Television.
[xv] Chung, Jen. The Gothamist, "Nicole DuFresne's Killer Sentenced to Life." Last modified December 12, 2006. Accessed May 2, 2012. http://gothamist.com/2006/12/12/nicole_dufresne.php.
[xvi] Burton William Peretti, *Nightclub City: Politics and Amusement in Manhattan*, (Philadelphia, PA: University of Pennsylvania Press, 2007), 125-131.
[xvii] David Carter, *Stonewall: The Riots That Sparked the Gay Revolution*, (New York City: St. Martin's Press, 2004).
[xviii] David Von Drehle, *Triangle: The Fire That Changed America*, (New York City: Grove Press, 2003).
[xix] Dan Berger, *Outlaws of America: The Weather Underground And the Politics of Solidarity*, (Oakland, CA: AK Press, 2006).
[xx] Joyce Johnson, *What Lisa Knew: The Truth and Lies of the Steinberg Case*, (New York City: Kensington Publishing Corporation, 1991).
[xxi] Quinion, Michael. "World Wide Words." Last modified June 24, 2000. Accessed May 2, 2012. http://www.worldwidewords.org/qa/qa-eig1.htm.
[xxii] Myron Peretz Glazer, and Penina Migdal Glazer, *The Whistleblowers: Exposing Corruption in Government and Industry*, (New York City: Basic Books, 1991).
[xxiii] Jerry Capeci, *Jerry Capeci's Gang Land, (*New York City: Penguin Group, 2003).
[xxiv] Raab, Selwyn. "Vincent Gigante, Mob Boss Who Feigned Incompetence to Avoid Jail, Dies at 77." *The New York Times*, December 20, 2005. http://www.nytimes.com/2005/12/20/obituaries/20gigante.html?pagewanted=all (accessed 2 May 2012).

[xxv] McFadden, Robert D. "RAMPAGE IN GREENWICH VILLAGE; In Heart of Village, 4 Lives Intersect in a Chain of Violence." *The New York Times*, March 16, 2007. http://query.nytimes.com/gst/fullpage.html?res=9402EFDE1F31F935A25750C0A9619C8B63&pagewanted=all (accessed 2 May, 2007).

[xxvi] Henry Paul Jeffers, *The 100 Greatest Heroes*, (New York City: Citadel Press, 2003), 215-217.

[xxvii] James Lardner, and Thomas Rappetto, *Nypd: A City and Its Police*, (New York City: Henry Holt & Co, 2000), 128-145.

xxviii Edwin G Burrows, and Mike Wallace, *Gotham: a history of New York City to 1898*, (New York City: Oxford University Press, 1999), 545-546.

[xxix] Coppola, Francis Ford, "The Godfather," Film.

[xxx] Coppola, Francis Ford. "The Godfather Part III." Film.

[xxxi] Jerry Capeci, *Jerry Capeci's Gang Land, (*New York City: Penguin Group, 2003).

[xxxii] Howard Blum, *Gangland: how the FBI broke the Mob*, (New York City: Simon & Schuster, 1993).

[xxxiii] Dwyer, Jim. "Publicity First, Evidence Later in Patz Arrest."*The New York Times*, May 25, 2012. http://www.nytimes.com/2012/05/25/nyregion/arrest-of-etan-patz-suspect-shows-haste-by-the-police.html (accessed 26 May 2012).

[xxxiv] Berman, Thomas, and Lauren Sher. ABC News, "Etan Patz Case Reopened 31 Years Later." Last modified May 26, 2010.

http://abcnews.go.com/2020/etan-patz-missing-boy-case-reopened-31-years/story?id=10749565
[xxxv] "CRIME: Death of a Maverick Mafioso." *TIME* , April 17, 1972.
[xxxvi] "Sun Sing Theatre." *LIFE*, May 1, 1950. http://books.google.com/books?id=-UwEAAAAMBAJ&printsec=frontcover
[xxxvii] NY Ago, "Florence (Sun Sing) Theatre." Accessed July 3, 2012. http://www.nycago.org/Organs/NYC/html/FlorenceTheatre.html.
[xxxviii] Daly, Michael. "Chinatown." *New York Magazine*, Feb 14, 1983. http://books.google.com/books?id=INgBAAAAMBAJ&pg=PA38&lpg=PA38&dq=Pagoda Theatre East Broadway&source=bl&ots=lsz4DiXh3d&sig=NZJisYIr8mPZa1vZUto60DQlDx8&hl=en&ei=mhGATZjcCMG1tgeC8szFCA&sa=X&oi=book_result&ct=result&resnum=8&ved=0CEYQ6AEwBw
[xxxix] Krcmarik, Katherine L. History of Tattooing, "Tattooing in the 1900s." Last modified April 2003. Accessed May 2, 2012.
[xl] Cliff White, *Flash from the Bowery: Classic American Tattoos, 1900-1950*, (Atglen, PA: Schiffer Pub Limited, 2011).
[xli] Ko-Lin Chin, *Chinatown Gangs: Extortion, Enterprise, and Ethnicity*, (New York City: Oxford University Press, 2000), 50.
[xlii] Patrick Radden Keefe, *The Snakehead: An Epic Tale of the Chinatown Underworld and the American Dream*, (New York City: Random House Digital, 2009), 75-76.
[xliii] Patrick Radden Keefe, The Snakehead: An Epic Tale of the Chinatown Underworld and the American Dream, (New York City: Random House Digital,

2009), 18-19.

[xliv] Jeffrey Scott McIllwain, *Organizing Crime In Chinatown: Race and Racketeering in New York City, 1890-1910*, (Jefferson, NC: McFarland & Co, 2003).
[xlv] Capeci, Jerry, and Ying Chan. "Gang Bosses' Betrayal Ghost Shadows Bigs Inform On Members." *New York Daily News*, October 27, 1996. http://articles.nydailynews.com/1996-10-27/news/18017768_1_gang-leader-ghost-shadows-big-brother (accessed 2 May 2012).
[xlvi] Carlo DeVito, *The Encyclopedia of International Organized Crime*, (New York City: Facts on File, Inc, 2005), 59.
[xlvii] Beverly Gage, *The Day Wall Street Exploded: A Story of America in Its First Age of Terror* , (New York City: Oxford University Press, 2009).
[xlviii] Dunlap, David W. "Old Station House Returns to Police Duty; Headquarters of First Precinct Until 1973 Will House the Police Museum." *The New York Times*, July 31, 2001. http://www.nytimes.com/2001/07/31/nyregion/old-station-house-returns-police-duty-headquarters-first-precinct-until-1973.html (accessed 2 May, 2012).
[xlix] Esther Singleton, *Historic buildings of America as seen and described by famous writers*, (New York City: Dodd, Mead & Co, 1906), 33-42.
[l] Martin, C. Gus, ed. *The SAGE Encyclopedia of Terrorism, Second Edition*. Thousand Oaks, CA: SAGE Publications, 2011. s.v. "FALN (Laura Lambert, writer)."
[li] Benedict, A.C. "Hope of Recovery." *Philadelphia Inquirer*, November 22, 2001.
[lii] Bernard Schwartz, *A History Of the Supreme Court*, (Oxford, UK: Oxford University Press, 1995).

[liii] Weege, Reinhold, "Night Court," 1984-1992, Television.
[liv] Coppola, Francis Ford, "The Godfather," Film.
[lv] Lumet, Sidney, "12 Angry Men," 1957, Film.
[lvi] Eaton, Leslie. "Russian Emigres Run Afoul of Stock Regulators." *The New York Times*, January 14, 1997.
[lvii] Levitt, Leonard. *NYPD Confidential: Power and Corruption in the Country's Greatest Police Force*. New York City: Macmillian, 2010.
[lviii] Robert L. Snow, *Technology and Law Enforcement: From Gumshoe to Gamma Rays*, (Westport, CT: Praeger Publishing, 2007), 82.
[lix] Wolf, Dick, "Law & Order: Criminal Intent." 2001-2011, Television.

[lx] Anne-Marie E Cantwell, and Diana iZerega Wall, *Unearthing Gotham: The Archaeology of New York City*, (New Haven, CT: Yale University Press, 2001), 278-294.
[lxi] George P Fletcher, *A Crime of Self-Defense: Bernhard Goetz and the Law on Trial*, (Chicago, IL: University of Chicago Press, 1990).
[lxii] Rayman, Graham, and Daryl Khan. Menace Turns to Murder / Encounters between Davis, Askew grew more chilling, "Newsday.com." Last modified July 24, 2003. Accessed May 2, 2012. http://www.newsday.com/news/menace-turns-to-murder-encounters-between-davis-askew-grew-more-chilling-1.473658.

23153379R00059

Made in the USA
Charleston, SC
14 October 2013